*Weeping may endure for a night but joy comes in the morning.*
*~Psalm 30:5b*

# UNEARNED
## *Grief*

~THE HEART'S JOURNEY FROM PAIN TO PEACE~

## KEVIN GERARD ELLISON, SR.

UNEARNED GRIEF: THE HEART'S JOURNEY FROM PAIN TO PEACE

KEVIN GERARD ELLISON, SR.

# Unearned Grief

## The Heart's Journey from Pain to Peace

Kevin Gerard Ellison, Sr.

*"Weeping may endure for a night but
joy comes in the morning."*
*~Psalm 30:5b*

UNEARNED GRIEF
Copyright © April 2021 by Kevin Gerard Ellison, Sr.
ISBN 978-1-7369125-0-8

Unless otherwise credited, all scripture references in this book come from the New King James Version (NKJV).

The description of the five stages of grief, mentioned in the epilogue, is used by permission of Ken Ross, President of EKR Foundation
http:// www.ekrfoundation.org
www.instagram.com/elisabethkublerross/
Graphic Designer: Tracy Spencer/Editor: Julie Boney
Publisher: Executive Business Writing

## In Memory of...

My beautiful daughter, Asheli Marie Ellison (1988-1990), and my precious son, Aaron Michael Ellison (1992-2012).

# Table of Contents

# Dedication

First and foremost, I dedicate this book to my Lord and Savior, Jesus Christ, for without Him I would be lost. Then, with a heart full of love, I would like to dedicate this book to my son—my first-born child—Kevin Gerard Ellison, Jr. I also give a special dedication of honor to my parents who have passed on, Francis Gerard Ellison (1925-2010), Mattie Louise (Ponder) Shannon (1929-2011), and stepfather, Earl E. Shannon. To the mother of my children, LeeAnn (Morris) Ellison, I also dedicate this book, as she and I share that unenviable pain of losing not one, but two children.

# Acknowledgements

I want to acknowledge my sister, Debra A. Jackson, and her children, Erika L. Bailey, Mieah L. Jackson, and Jerran J. Jackson, all of our cousins, uncles, aunts, the host of relatives and loved ones who have been called home, friends, and co-workers in the tire industry with me. I want to thank Rhonda E. L. Lattimore and family, my church families, my powerful leaders in the Grief Ministry at the Way World Outreach, and my wife, Karen (Seward) Ellison, for being with me during the time of Aaron's loss and the court proceedings. Thanks also go to my daughter, Isabel Ruvalcaba, for her diligence in helping to edit and format, and to Carla Capelo, who started the editing process. To everyone who reads *Unearned Grief*, may you all be blessed by this reading.

# Introduction

Every day in life the human race can experience the pain of death. We will grieve the loss of someone dear to us. Grief will often bring unbearable emotional feelings associated with loss. Grief will try to run away from you and your ability to heal. Grief can be a heavy weight placed upon our shoulders. I write this book to let humanity know that we can heal from grief. We don't have to be bound by grief, nor hide behind it, and the heaviness can be lifted off or we can gain strength to not let it bear us down.

I have been brought through a journey of grief that started in 1990 and occurred again in 2012. Those were very significant years to me with the loss of my two children, Asheli and Aaron. On this road, I have found that it can be very lonely if you travel it on your own, trying to heal. Alone, all you do is bury it. My prayer and desire are for us to learn to deal with our grief by allowing God to guide and help us in this journey, to bring us into healing from the pain of grief. This will never be an overnight journey or a quick fix. It's a process that only God will carry us through, as He did for me and countless others from the Grief Ministry at our church.

As you read this book, realize that I am human just like you are, with pain and heartache from the loss of loved ones.

Introduction

But in Psalm 121:1-2, we read, "**I will lift up my eyes to the hills – From whence comes my help? My help** *comes* **from the Lord, Who made heaven and earth.**" (KJV) This is who will guide us and take us on this step-by-step journey into healing. We have to be willing to let God heal us. He is so instrumental in why I wrote this. I will never forget my children, but I now look at their names and their memories without my mind being cluttered by the dark clouds of grief. It now has become a refreshed ray of sunlight into their memory. Please come and join God's healing.

# Preface

To begin the story of my first encounter with unearned grief, I must start with my 2-year-old daughter Asheli. Though this was a very tough time in my life for where I was mentally, physically, and spiritually, in the midst of this tragedy, God's hands were with me.

### Asheli Marie Ellison

It was a difficult time in my life. I was separated from the mother of my children, LeeAnn, and was living in Santa Ana, at a friend's house. LeeAnn, Kevin Jr., and Asheli were living in our apartment in Yorba Linda. At a family function, my sister offered to watch Kevin Jr. (4years old) and Asheli (2 years old) during the work week, and either LeeAnn or I would pick them up on the weekends to come home. My sister felt this would help us during the time of our separation. It would be less of a burden on us. We agreed. During this time, I lent my mind and thoughts completely over to the separation. I felt this marriage was over, and that I could do what I wanted. I dated other women and I didn't care, since I was separated.

I was in control of my thoughts and actions (or so I thought), and of course I was drinking alcohol to hide my pain and bitterness. A lot. I was using sex and alcohol to escape from the pain of my separation, and I was selfishly thinking of myself. I knew deep inside I wasn't living right, being brought up in the church, but at this time I was following after other influences that had me bound.

I was spending a Friday night at this woman's house, and during my sleep that evening I had a terrible dream about Asheli. In the dream I saw her floating face down in a Jacuzzi pool. I awoke to a yell from within my deep sleep. I was very startled and nervous because of what this dream was implying about my daughter. I was afraid to tell anyone about it. LeeAnn dropped Kevin Jr. and Asheli off at my sister's house on the Monday following the dream I had on Friday.

On Tuesday while I was working, I received a call from my mother to come to Riverside, "Kevin, call LeeAnn and both of you come to Riverside. There has been an accident, and Kevin Jr. ..." I said, "What about Kevin Jr.? "Momma, what happened?" She replied, "You guys just come here. We are at Riverside Community Hospital." I immediately called LeeAnn and told her something had happened, I didn't know what, and that we needed to go to Riverside immediately. I went and picked LeeAnn up and we drove to Riverside. All kinds of thoughts were racing through my mind. "Oh my God, what has happened to my son? Please Lord, what has happened?"

We arrived at the hospital and went into the emergency room. As we turned the corner, I saw Kevin Jr. run towards us in his socks. These next words are seared into my memory and heart. My mother said, "Kevin, it's not Kevin Jr.; it's Asheli. She is gone!" I said, "What, What! What do you mean, she's gone!" LeeAnn immediately fell to the ground and shouted, "Oh no! Not my baby!" What happened? We were told there was a fire at my sister's house that day. My sister has three children of her own, and they were all being put down to take a nap. Asheli loved to sleep on the floor. Even at the apartment, when she was in bed she would get out and lay on the floor to sleep. I was told that when a plug was pulled out of the wall socket it flashed, and a piece of wallpaper caught on fire and the room was engulfed in smoke and heat. She had perished from smoke inhalation. All the other children survived.

The hospital was full of family; the pastor from the Kansas Ave. Church was there to talk to and console us. There were also some of my mother's immediate friends from church who had come when the news had gone out about the tragedy.

The days after experiencing the loss of Asheli weighed so much on me. First the dream and now the realization of what had happened. I didn't blame God. Who I blamed was me! I was guilty of adultery. I knew better. I even told God that if He would get me through, that I would help others to know Him. I spoke it, but at that time alcohol and anger were my driving force. I wanted revenge for Asheli's death. I wanted this hurt and pain to go away.

## Preface

LeeAnn and I reconciled. We received an insurance claim for the loss of Asheli. I was transferred to a tire franchise in Corona, California. We bought a home in the Corona area. I would go to work every day, not really caring about anyone. Anger had a foothold on me, revenge had its grip on me, and the drinking had now gone to a new level of addiction. All I could imagine was how was I going to transfer this pain and hurt to someone else so I would feel better. I thought this was my answer—hurt somebody so I wouldn't hurt so much. These thoughts flooded by alcohol were convincing me this was the road to take. Every day as customers would come to the counter looking for tires or service, I would say within myself, "Are you the one who's going to piss me off today so I can release this anger and get the peace I am looking for?"

I had these thoughts every day, and at the end of my workday, the drinking of alcohol would fuel the rage. I even imagined grabbing someone by the neck and separating their head from their body. My frame of thought was that I had to do just enough to make sure business met its goals to keep my job, but I had no compassion or feelings for anyone because of the anger and pain raging inside of me. Somehow this had to be released. I was burying Asheli's death and my feeling of being the cause of her death.

This went on for months. Then one day it happened. A mechanic at the shop came to me about 9:30 am and asked if he could go home since he wasn't feeling very well. With no compassion of feelings, I said, "No, go back to work." At 11:00 am he returned and said, "Kevin, I really don't feel well; can I go home?" I replied again, "No. You have to finish the car." I had no feelings at all. Then about 2:00 pm he returned and said, "I really need to go home. No way that customer needs their car!" As he was turning away from me, he uttered these words, "You stupid Nigger!" That was it! The volcano was about to erupt. All that bottled up anger, hate, pain, revenge, and the thought of grabbing him by the throat and pulling his head from his body were coming to fruition. I felt the rage start at my feet and as it rose, this pressure was gaining force. I felt it hit my waist to my chest; it went to my head then down to my arms. My hands opened wide in a cupped motion to grab his neck, and as I leaped to grab him, all of a sudden my body completely froze. It was paralyzed. I could not move a muscle. Just as fast as the rage and pain had risen up inside of me it had turned to immediate peace. Something or Someone had taken complete control because all that pain was gone. I looked into my employee's eyes and I saw his pain, what he was going through. I immediately said to him, "Go home and get better." I turned around and headed back into the showroom and put my arm up on the counter and said, "What was that, and what just happened?"

# Preface

That was God allowing me to experience His presence in my life. He was answering what I had asked Him earlier about helping others to come to know Him. God was faithful no matter how messed up I was or what state of mind, or condition I was in. I know He had been with me during the loss of Asheli. I hadn't given my heart back to God yet, but it was coming.

Philippians 1:6 says, **"I am convinced and confident of this very thing, that He who has begun a good work in you will [continue to] perfect and complete it until the day of Christ Jesus [the time of His return]."** (AMP) I also believe in Romans 5:8: **"But God demonstrates His own love toward us, in that while we were still sinners, Christ died for us."** I know God had forgiven me for my sins, the sin of adultery. I was learning that God is sovereign.

In 1992 my son Aaron was born, and on April 24, 1994, God completely delivered me from my alcohol addiction. I had now become a single father, raising my sons, and I didn't want them exposed to alcohol. I thank God for deliverance. As this book continues, it will show God's faithfulness to us in the continued journey from my heart's *pain* to *peace*.

# Chapter 1

# The Sting of Death II

Every day we wake up planning our day—things we have to get accomplished, places we have to travel. We, unfortunately, don't possess the ability to see what each day's outcome will be. That only comes by our all-knowing God. I did not know, or expect, that soon I would be acquainted with *unearned grief* and the process of God helping me heal from it. Thursday, January 19, 2012, would be the last day I would see my youngest son alive. The next time I would see Aaron he would be lying in a casket.

That morning I suggested, "Let's go to the barber and get haircuts," because we both looked like shaggy dawgs. We lived in Temecula, California at the time. I took him to the barbershop, and after the cuts were done I was so impressed with how Aaron's cut showed what a very handsome son he was. I made sure he knew that the barber had done an excellent job cutting and grooming his hair. At the time I said, "Man, it's tapered so good. Your goatee. The hairline. Don't be flirtin' with all them girls at school!"

Then, while driving home, Aaron said, "Hey Dad, I want to go for the job interview on Monday." Earlier that week, I had told Aaron about one of my customers who was a warehouse manager looking for workers. Aaron had also set up a counseling appointment at Chaparral High School to talk to his counselor about finishing his studies for his diploma. I agreed that was a great idea. He was looking to prepare himself for his future: education—check, appearance—check, and employment—check. My heart leaped with joy!

On Friday, I left for work at my tire franchise located in Lake Elsinore, California. Aaron would sometimes come and work there on the weekends. When I got home from work that evening, I asked Kevin Jr., my oldest son, if he had seen Aaron that day. He said he had, and that Aaron had gone out with friends for the evening. The next morning, I looked into Aaron's room and saw that he hadn't made it home. I asked Kevin Jr. if he had heard from Aaron. Kevin responded that Aaron called the night before and told him he was staying at a friend's house. I got dressed for church and left. Later that afternoon, when I got home from church in Riverside, I asked Kevin if Aaron had made it home. He explained that Aaron had come home, showered, changed his clothes, and was going to a house party with friends. It was Saturday late in the afternoon; I still hadn't seen Aaron since Thursday. As that evening came to a close, I fell asleep around 10 pm. Suddenly, I was awakened out of a deep, sound sleep. Immediately, I rolled out of bed onto my knees, kneeled next to my bed, and started to call out my son's name, *"Aaron."* "Lord God, I don't know what is happening, but I pray that your arms of protection will be with Aaron." I prayed and called out his name.

At the time, I didn't know why I awoke from my sleep. I strained to read the clock; it was 2:48 in the morning. (You will understand the significance of this later.) So, I got back into the bed and dozed off. My alarm went off at 6:30 am. It was time to get ready for work. I got out of bed, went to Aaron's room to see if he was there, and to wake him up to go to work with me. His bed hadn't been touched or slept in. A sense of uneasiness came over me. I felt darkness inside of me. After showering and getting dressed for work I headed downstairs. I opened the front door to find a business card that had been wedged in the door. I watched it as it fluttered to the ground, as if in slow motion. It landed face up. That was when I saw the words "Sheriff Department." I turned it over and found instructions to call the number on the front of the card. I got this eerie feeling inside my stomach.

I wondered, *What has happened?*

I got into my vehicle and proceeded to get to work, reluctant to make this call. But I did it anyway.

"Sheriff's department. How can I help you?" Someone greeted me in a detached voice.

"My name is Kevin Ellison," I offered before adding, "I found this card on my door."

She inquired, "Do you have a son named Aaron Ellison?"

" Yes," I said.

"I hate to be the one to tell you, but he was involved in a car accident last night, and he didn't make it."

"What?" I said. "What are you talking about?"

I had stopped in the middle of the street in total disbelief. I started driving, turning and heading back to my house to tell his brother Kevin what I had just been informed of. When I approached our home, Kevin was coming outside to go to work. He also worked with me at our tire franchise.

I said, "Kevin, Aaron was in an accident last night and he didn't make it. He's gone."

Kevin immediately fell to his knees in disbelief, brokenhearted, and started to cry. "I've already lost a little sister, and now my little brother."

All that was going through my mind was *Why Lord? Why?* This is *my* second child that *we* had lost. *Why?*

I said, "Kevin, I need to go to the shop and tell them we are not going to work today."

I immediately called the family to tell them what had happened. Upon arriving at my tire store, I walked into the showroom office and saw a fellow member of church who had come to get service on his vehicle. When our eyes met, I knew he saw the pain in mine. He asked what was wrong. I told him that Aaron had been killed in a car accident the night before and I wasn't going to be at work that day.

I told my fellow workers what happened. They all knew Aaron because of his time spent at the shop on the weekends working. They all gave us their condolences as we were leaving.

As I talked, I felt such an emptiness from the loss of Aaron; now the sting of death had struck again.

Psalm 61:1-2: **"O God, listen to my cry! Hear my prayer! From the ends of the earth, I cry to you for help when my heart is overwhelmed. Lead me to the towering rock of safety."** (NLT)

Matthew 5:4: **"Blessed are those who mourn, for they shall be comforted."**

The Sting of Death II

# Chapter 2

# A Still Small Voice

As Kevin Jr.. and I drove to Riverside, the emptiness and overwhelming feeling of loss tugged at my heart, mind, and soul. I was breaking inside. I remembered how I had felt the day I lost my daughter in a house fire. That same hurt and pain now doubled inside of me. I was hurting.

Looking over at my oldest son, Kevin Jr., it dawned on me he was now my only child. I teared even more. I prayed nothing would ever happen to him. There was complete silence in my car as we made the ride to Riverside from Lake Elsinore. It was a dark, empty, and lonely ride.

We arrived at my sister's house. Family members who had already arrived gathered outside on the driveway. They came and embraced Kevin Jr. and me. We all had tears in our eyes with disbelief, especially my sister's son, Jerran. He and Aaron were peas in a pod, joined from the hip. He was taking this news very hard about his cousin, as was my sister Debra.

Aaron had spent a lot of time at my sister's house. She was like a second mother to him. I saw so much pain in her face, which was coming from her heart. She loved Aaron as a son of her own.

That is when I took off walking down the street by myself. As I cried, I yelled to God, "Why God? Why? Why? This is my second child who has died. Why? Why did he have to die also? Please help me understand this, Lord. Please!"

As I rounded the corner, more family members and friends had shown up to my sister's house to offer condolences for our loss. Clergy from our church came to pray with the family; other friends brought food and lots of love to pour on us that day.

Later that evening we drove back to the house in Temecula. It was a very long, dark, and dreary ride. Emptiness welled up inside me as I turned into the driveway. Looking up at Aaron's bedroom window, all I saw was darkness. Tears rolled down my face.

After entering the house, I went straight to Aaron's room. Glancing about, I realized I would never see him again. I felt the pain of grief welling up inside of me. I stood there and just starring at the emptiness in his room.

I decided I wasn't going to touch anything in his room. Later, I would often go into his room just to lift up his blanket and bring it up to my nose to smell his scent. I would look around, remembering how I often told him to clean up this room. Now, all I wanted was for him to be alive and well. I would now be missing out on his triumphs and his mishaps as he navigated being a young teenager growing into manhood. I would not witness him achieve his dreams. Kevin Jr. also was going through a lot of pain. I will share that in a later chapter.

The next day was even harder. The loss of a child was taking a toll on me as I was trying to understand why that had happened. Aaron was the second child I lost. I lost my daughter Asheli M. Ellison when she was 2 years old, tragically. I was at a loss. But I do thank God for the relationship that I had with Him. Romans 8:16: **"The Spirit Himself bears witness with our spirit that we are children of God."** Also in Romans 9:1: **"I tell the truth in Christ, I am not lying, my conscience also bearing me witness in the Holy Spirit."**

Later that evening I heard in my heart from the Spirit of God, what I will never forget, **"Saturday, be in church for that is where you will find your strength."**

I believe God knew all this was going to happen in my life. God's presence was being poured into my life. My relationship with Jesus is what I needed during this time.

A few days after Aaron passed, a lot of his friends arranged to have a vigil for him. We were to meet at Harveston, a housing community by the lake in Temecula, bringing candles to fellowship and to pray.

Jeremiah 29:13: **"You will seek me and find me when you seek me with all your heart."**

# A Still Small Voice

# Chapter 3

## The Road to Peace

Going through my mind was that I lost my father in 2010, lost my mother in 2011, and now three months later, my youngest son. The Saturday after Aaron's untimely passing, I went to church as the Spirit had told me to do. Church members embraced me with love and prayers of comfort. The head elder, a father with a son, came and grabbed my hand and led me to a quiet place in the church. With tears flowing from his eyes, he asked if he could pray for me. Another father came up to me and gave me a note with scriptures of healing, peace, and comfort.

During the sermon, I stood up in the middle of the pew, tears rolling down my face. A fellow member came down from the balcony to embrace and hug me. She stayed there with me until a calming set in.

In the days to come I experienced the heavy grief of losing my son. As the pain of loss for my son welled up inside, I had to gasp to catch my breath.

I cried out to God, "Lord please help me. I'm going through this. I need you now. Lord, please give me peace. I need you!"

11

The Road to Peace

As soon as I pleaded for the Lord's help, a supernatural peace came over me. My mind traveled to a place of comfort. Time after time, I experienced this overwhelming bout with grief, and then I would become confident in the faithful promise of the Holy Spirit to take me into a place of God's peace.

In Psalm 34:18, we are told, **"The LORD is close to the brokenhearted; He rescues those whose spirits are crushed." (NLT)** I became more and more dependent on the presence of God's Spirit to help and guide me during this time of grief. Whenever I called on the Lord, the Spirit of God would always be there to help lead me out of the pains of grief—no matter what I was experiencing. I didn't realize this was the beginning of God's process on my path of healing. He would be taking me step by step through the process of healing. I just had to be obedient to the Spirit's prompting to hear His voice.

As a matter of fact, I was prompted to drive out to the place of the accident where the car had rolled, and he had been ejected. Looking on the ground and seeing the fresh marks on the dirt and disfigured bushes, I spotted something: a package of candy that Aaron loved to eat. A forgotten bag of Trolli (a sweet and sour candy), lay on the ground unopened. I also found one of his shoes. The force of the impact from being thrown through the windshield must have dislodged Aaron's body from this very shoe. This shoe that I held was now very precious to me. I picked up both articles, the Trolli candy, and Aaron's loafer. As I stood there, giving the crash site one last look, I knew it was God who had given me enough strength to make the trip to the site. As painful as it was, He led me through it. To this day, whenever I see Trolli candy, it reminds me of him.

# The Road to Peace

# Chapter 4

## Grief and the Grave

Aaron's funeral was scheduled to be held on Saturday, February 4, 2012. Up to that day, our time was mostly spent trying not to think of that day. I was trying to keep my mind occupied to keep it off his funeral. It seems like there is a large space or a vast place of emptiness between the day of his passing up until the funeral.

The mortuary had to go with a preliminary death certificate for Aaron's funeral because the autopsy results had not come in yet. I felt anxious and unsettled not knowing the exact cause of his death. Was it blunt force trauma? Did he break his neck? Had he experienced a lot of pain—if so, for how long? Were drugs, alcohol or even foul play involved? Somehow, I thought if I had the official report, it would help bring closure. However, we proceeded without the it. I supplied the mortuary with Aaron's shoe and his bag of Trolli candy that I had found at the crash site. The funeral was all set.

Thinking about the funeral, the day our loved one would be laid to rest, can cause one to feel a heaviness in their heart and spirit. You could feel like you don't want to go on. I felt that way. It's on that day that we realize that we will never see our loved one again on this side of Heaven.

Grief and the Grave

My youngest son was no longer with us. Not hearing his distinct laugh left a void in our lives. He loved comedies. The Office was one of his favorites. We could hear him laughing from outside the house/the TV room/his room. He also loved cooking and he watched cooking shows every chance he got because he wanted to become a chef.

I was impressed to pray, "Lord, please don't let my son's death be in vain. I pray that lives might be changed because of his death. Please Lord, hear my cry." I would offer this prayer every day.

His funeral was held at Kansas Avenue Church in Riverside, California. The family had met in a secluded room inside the church before the service was to begin. The officiating pastor, Bron Jacobs, led us in prayer while the church was filling up. As we got up, we were led down to the front pews where the casket of Aaron was positioned. We sat down and the service started.

The opening prayer was led by Pastor Ruben Rios. Songs were performed by special guest singers. One of my favorite songs was sung by Apostle Duane Spencer, "Praise Is What I Do." After this song, Pastor Jacobs delivered a powerful eulogy. I believe it was sent down from Heaven for my son's service, as well as the prayer which I had been praying up until Aaron's funeral, that his death would not be in vain, and lives could be changed.

Pastor Jacobs asked me to come down to the front and to stand in front of Aaron's casket. I turned around to face the congregation and what I saw captivated my heart. The large church was full, from top to bottom. There was not a seat left in the balcony. I marveled at the realization that Aaron touched so many lives. I believe that a lot of those people came to support the family. So many came from Temecula's Chaparral High School: teachers, classmates, and parents.

Pastor Jacobs made a call to the congregation to stand and come down front. "If any of you want to accept Jesus Christ into your life, come and touch Aaron's father."

I raised my hand as I would to shake someone's hand. They came and touched my hand in agreement with the pastor's call. I saw young teenagers, one after another, standing to their feet to come down to the altar to say "yes" to Jesus. It was so overwhelming. They were coming down, tears streaming down their faces. Tears were streaming down my face seeing child after child coming to receive Jesus. At one point it seemed like it wasn't going to stop. Unspeakable joy swelled up in my heart as I witnessed this miracle.

John 12:24: **"I tell you the truth, unless a kernel of wheat is planted in the soil and dies, it remains alone. But its death will produce many new kernels—a plentiful harvest of new lives."** (NLT)

I saw my prayer being answered. God's process of healing—in the midst of grieving—was being administered. Sometimes we don't see Him in the midst of our pain, but God was surely there, His presence being planted into the lives of Aaron's classmates. On the Monday following the funeral, we laid Aaron to rest with his sister, Asheli, at Olivewood Cemetery in Riverside.

A couple of weeks later, my eldest son, Kevin Jr., and I were invited to Chaparral High School for an assembly on the effects of driving while intoxicated, sponsored by M.A.D.D. After M.A.D.D had done their presentation, I was asked to address the students in the gym—most of whom were Aaron's friends and classmates.

I asked them to look to their left and tell that person that they were special; then turn and look to the right and tell that person that they were special, too. I affirmed that every student was loved and very special. I reminded them that if anyone told them that they weren't going to measure up to anything, that was a lie. I went on to tell the story of Aaron, of how special he was—not perfect—but special.

I added, "You will get out of life what you put into it. Be positive, and have positive words spoken over you. You will succeed at anything you put your minds to do."

At the end, my son, Kevin, got up before the assembled students and gave them something to remember: Aaron's laugh. They stood and applauded us.

*Another step in the process of healing: positive words.*

Grief and the Grave

## Chapter 5

## Guilt and Anger—"Who's Responsible?"

I remained as busy as I could; it had been a little over a month since Aaron had passed away. What made it so hard was waiting for the finalization of the coroner's report before getting a death certificate. It seemed like a lifetime had passed while we waited for the information about how and what caused Aaron's death. I would call periodically to inquire from the coroner's office; they told me they were waiting for the toxicology report to help finalize the findings. You can imagine our family's experience of grieving and what was going through our minds during this process of waiting.

One afternoon I got the call that the report was finished, and I could come and get it. I was reluctant to go get the report, but my wife, Karen, convinced me to go and get it. As I drove to Perris, California to get the report and pulled into the parking lot, a memory flashed back to me on the Sunday, the day of Aaron's passing, how we drove down here to the coroner's office. I wanted to go and see his body and they wouldn't let me or the family in. Now I was back in this place with the memory of death that surrounds this facility. As I was sitting in the office, a deputy came and acknowledged me and led me to a conference room.

The deputy handed me the report. I pulled it out of the envelope while she retained her copy. She explained why this took so long. The office had to rule out other possible causes—questions like, "Was there foul play?" "Did he die at the hands of others?" "Was it chemical or did his body sustain traumatic injury?" All causes had to be exhausted to finalize the report. What came out of her mouth next caused my heart to stop for a few seconds. "We can't find anything that caused the death of Aaron." The office is labeling it "unknown causes," meaning they couldn't find the cause of his death.

I thought about what the investigating highway patrolman said to me in his report of when Aaron was ejected from the vehicle when it rolled, and that when it landed, the vehicle's tire was about one to two feet away from his head, and that he had been ejected through the front windshield, and upon his landing on the ground there was no evidence of any broken bones or any deep cuts or lacerations from going through the windshield.

I said to the deputy that if nothing at the accident caused his death and the coroner's office couldn't find anything, it dawns on me it had to be the hand of God written all over this. I imagined that while I was praying at the moment of this accident, God sent His angels to hold him as he was ejected, and to protect and lay him down to sleep in Christ on the ground. Aaron's only injury was a small cut on his wrist. I've spoken to but a very few about these findings, but I know God is always with us, even in a time of death.

On the night Aaron passed, he was with people he had just met, coming from a party, and traveling on a dark road in Temecula, heading back to the party. Aaron and three other occupants were in the car. A young lady was driving, Aaron in the passenger seat, and two males occupied the back seats. Under the influence of alcohol, the driver's reflexes were impaired. When someone shouted for her to look out, she swerved to avoid a collision with an oncoming vehicle. Instead, the car flipped and rolled. My son Aaron was ejected. Unfortunately, he wasn't wearing his seatbelt. The others survived the accident.

When the Highway Patrol, police, and ambulance arrived on the scene, they administered an alcohol test and found the driver's alcohol level was well over the legal limit. The district attorney was called to the scene. Because the accident resulted in a fatality, the driver was arrested.

As I mentioned in Chapter 1, on January 22nd I was awakened, and I fell to my knees praying and calling out Aaron's name to God at 2:48 am—the exact time as the events connected with the accident took place.

## Guilt and Anger—"Who's Responsible?"

The district attorney's office contacted me soon after the accident to talk me through the process of someone losing their life at the hands of another. As I sat in the DA's office, they presented me with the reasons I should seek the maximum penalty. The charge of involuntary manslaughter while driving under the influence of alcohol would send her to jail for 12 years. Even at that moment, God had placed compassion in my heart for her. Her life would never be the same, as our lives would not be the same. My son had chosen to ride with them. I am not making light of this ordeal. I love and miss my son, but I asked the D.A. to seek a sentence of 2 years in jail and 2 years of probation. If she were ever caught drinking and driving, she would immediately serve the maximum of her sentence. My choice might have angered members of my family who believed that I should have requested the maximum sentence because she was the cause of Aaron's death. I felt I did the right thing.

On the first day of trial, a lot of family members showed up in court. Their stares threw daggers at the driver. Their anger at the loss of Aaron's life was evident. I bet her family expected a violent reaction from me and my family. I saw that a lot of members of her family had come to expect the worst. But God's presence was in my heart and in the courtroom that day.

As the judge concluded the proceedings on the last day at court, she asked me if I had anything to say to the defendant before she passed sentencing.

I replied, "Yes, Your Honor, I do." Standing, I turned and faced the driver and offered, "Ashley, I forgive you."

Karen later told me that she saw Ashley's shoulders drop at that point.

The judge asked Aaron's mother, LeeAnn, "Do you have anything to say?"

LeeAnn also said, "I forgive you."

While passing sentence, the judge reminded everyone how Ashley's choice to drive under the influence had changed the lives of Aaron's parents, as well as her own. The sight of the judge crying as she spoke her sentence will be forever branded into my memory and in my heart. She concluded by stating that after being released, Ashley would be compelled to give back under the stipulations of her probation. She would have to tell others about the dangers of driving intoxicated.

*Forgiveness is a powerful weapon that destroys the effects of anger and guilt.*

God was in this process of healing that he would reveal to me. Colossians 3:13: **"Make allowance for each other's faults and forgive anyone who offends you. Remember, the Lord forgave you, so you must forgive others."** (NLT)

Matthew 6:14: **"For if you forgive other people when they sin against you, your heavenly Father will also forgive you."** (KJV)

Guilt and Anger—"Who's Responsible?"

After a while, I started feeling a strong sense of guilt. It was my fault that my son had died. If I had been a better father raising him, he would not have been in that position to lose his life. I convinced myself I had seen the signs but ignored them. I reminded myself how I rationalized that Aaron would grow out of them, just like I did when I was young. God had delivered me, so He would do it for Aaron also.

He never got that chance, so I pressed myself into feeling more guilty over his death. Not seeing him alive before his passing added to it. The fact I never had the chance to say goodbye, or that I loved him, increased the guilt.

"Lord, I need you. Please, help me," I would say in my mind.

One night as I was sleeping, I had a very distinct dream of Aaron. In that dream, he came to me.

He said, "Daddy, I just came to tell you goodbye, and I love you."

I woke up to a sense of peace. Guilt had released its grip on my heart.

I found out that Kevin Jr., my eldest son, held in guilt for years over his brother's death. Kevin saw Aaron on Saturday afternoon when Aaron came home to change his clothes to go out for that evening.

He asked Kevin Jr., "Can I use your ID? There's a party at Pechanga and I want to go."

Kevin replied, "No! You're not getting busted, and my ID will get confiscated."

That decision weighed so heavily upon Kevin Jr. He often wondered if he had agreed to his brother's request, maybe he would not have gone to that party and he would still be here. This guilt was unbearable at times for Kevin Jr. to handle. I told him I was going to arrange counseling with the senior pastor at The Way World Outreach, Marco Garcia. Kevin came to church one Sunday, and after service he met with Pastor Marco. I wanted to go be there with him, but the Spirit said he needed to do this by himself. I introduced him to Pastor Marco and left. About two and a half hours later, my son walked up to me, his eyes bloodshot, evidence of his crying and state of mind. Kevin locked eyes with me and whispered, "I felt a weight fall off my shoulders."

His words will live forever in my heart.

"Praise God," I replied.

The burden of guilt had been lifted from both of us.

### *God's path is the path to heal.*

Matthew 11:28, 29: **"Then Jesus said, "Come to me, all of you who are weary and carry heavy burdens, and I will give you rest. Take my yoke upon you. Let me teach you, because I am humble and gentle at heart, and you will find rest for your souls."** (NLT)

Guilt and Anger—"Who's Responsible?"

# Chapter 6

# Enlightenment

Months passed after the funeral, and I still would have to call upon the Lord sometimes to get me through a time of grief. I would start to question, "Why God, why?" Some nights, lying in bed, I wondered, "Why did this happen?" I go to church, I am a Christian, I believe in Jesus, but doubt would often come.

One day, the Spirit impressed upon me to read the story of Uriah, the husband of Bathsheba, who was killed by King David over the king's lust for Bathsheba. Even though this is a tragic story of sin and God's forgiveness, it was through this lineage of David's and Bathsheba's union that Christ would come. Uriah's life was a sacrifice for our Lord and Savior to come into this world for our salvation. I was reminded that at Aaron's funeral so many of his classmates had given their lives to Christ. His life was instrumental for the seed of God to be planted in their hearts. God impressed in my heart that Aaron's assignment on this earth was for those nineteen years. His life was sacrificed for the many.

Sometimes, I would ask, "Why him, Lord? Why did I have to lose my youngest son?" But as I remembered those faces coming to accept Jesus Christ, my heart was healed from doubt. Knowing my son was now resting in Jesus consoled my heart. This was another road that God used for my healing. God still had more to guide me through.

We ended up hiring an attorney to pursue a wrongful death case against the family that knowingly allowed minors to drink alcohol the night Aaron died. The attorney summoned everyone who was involved in providing alcohol to the driver on that Saturday. My attorney told me that two males and another female accompanied the driver earlier in the day to purchase and drink alcohol. The attorney was showing the acts of the driver and passengers that contributed to the facts of the case to pursue or implicate them in the wrongful death lawsuit. After the lawsuit was completed, the two plaintiffs and Aaron's mother and I were awarded the proceeds from the insurance claim against the family that had provided alcohol at the party that evening.

One day a man knocked on our door. He said he was sorry for our loss, then handed me what appeared to be a sympathy card. In fact, it was a demand that I reimburse him for the money he had to spend for an attorney to represent his daughter who had been summoned by my attorney. She was one of the passengers who had been in the vehicle earlier that Saturday. I was devastated. I found out he had looked for me at my old place of employment, and my current place as well. He said some blasphemous words about my son and me. I became incredibly angry about this invasion of privacy, but I left it alone and gave it over to God. I'm sure I will hear from him once this book is published, but it is all about God's glory.

I was going through different emotional thoughts while I was working in Lake Elsinore at the tire franchise. I imagined myself riding a new Harley Davidson motorcycle; in fact, I wanted one. The gentleman, Sonny, who came biweekly to clean and polish the showroom floors had a beautiful red Harley Davidson motorcycle on which he would ride by on the weekends. That's what caused me to want to get a Harley Davidson. Sometime after, I inquired if he knew anyone who was selling one, and asked him to please let me know if he came across a good deal. Karen and I would go to different Harley dealerships on the weekends just to sit, and I would dream about owning and riding one.

One day when Sonny came by to do the floors, he mentioned that he met someone selling a Harley Davidson Softail Classic motorcycle at a really good price. The seller and I made arrangements to meet at his house in Riverside so I could see it. I was looking to purchase a Harley Davidson Road Glide or the Electric Glide Ultra Classic. When we arrived at Sonny's house, the sellers were there with family. When I saw the Harley, I said to myself, "I want it; I hope the price is in my budget." The seller and I agreed to a price that was good for both of us. I asked why they were selling it. She replied that her husband had a stroke and the doctor told him he couldn't ride it anymore. Before I could take ownership, the owner and I arranged to meet at her place of business to finalize the paperwork and get the pink slip.

While at her place of business, we started talking about family. I asked her how her husband was doing. "He's getting better," she said. Then I asked about her family. She told me that her family was involved in a sandwich restaurant business in Riverside; it's a business that has been in their family for years. She also talked to me about her daughter and her life's struggles, and as a parent, how hard it is to see your child go through struggles. I said I would pray for her. She asked, "How's your family? Do you have any children?" I replied that I had three children and that my daughter passed away in 1990 and my son passed away just three years ago in 2012, and it was because of the lawsuit that I was able to purchase the Harley Davidson from her. "This purchase will always have a special meaning," I said. We discussed how in life there are always circumstances we don't understand, and there will be times we will get an understanding. I told her how we had to go to court and how the court found the driver guilty and about how, in my heart, I forgave the driver. And at that moment the Lord revealed something to me. He said, "Remember all the times you called on My name to deliver you from the pains of grief? When you would call, 'Lord help me. I'm going through it!' and

My peace would come upon you, it was because you had forgiveness. It opened the door to your heart that I came through. It allowed Me access to you and your healing from grief."

Unforgiveness hinders God from accessing your heart. It blocks and delays healing. Allowing unforgiveness is like trying to put gas in your car with the gas cap on, and the gas pouring all over the car and ground instead. You try to get healing poured into you, but it has no clear path to your heart. Forgiving removes the cap, and allows the flow from God into you to bring you to a place of healing. This is what the Lord revealed to me.

*Having forgiveness in my heart gave me a new identity in healing from grief.*

Isaiah 55:8-9: **"My thoughts are nothing like your thoughts,"** says the Lord. **"And my ways are far beyond anything you could imagine. For just as the heavens are higher than the earth, so my ways are higher than your ways and my thoughts higher than your thoughts."** (NLT)

God is sovereign in all that He does. We may not know where the road ends up, but God is in control. We can be assured to trust in His ways. Healing is His will for us.

Psalm 28:7: **"The LORD is my strength and shield. I trust him with all my heart. He helps me, and my heart is filled with joy. I burst out in songs of thanksgiving. "** (NLT)

# Enlightenment

# Chapter 7

# Reflection of God's Grace

After my daughter's untimely passing, I was full of hate, revenge, and alcohol. I reacted to the pain of losing her by blaming myself. One day, I had a disagreement with a fellow employee and lunged at him. In truth, I was looking to extract my revenge on the unbearable pain I carried. Filled with anger, I tried to separate his head from his body, as if that could placate my grief. At that exact moment when I moved to hurt him, a supernatural presence came over me, and stopped me in my tracks. I froze. Unable to move, I surrendered to the heavenly peace that possessed me. Staring into that employee's eyes, the pain I was causing him reflected back at me.

Thus, I was introduced to the presence of the Holy Spirit. On April 24, 1994, the Holy Spirit urged me to call my cousin, who is a pastor. I asked him to come and see me. I was sick and tired of being sick and tired. I wanted Jesus back into my life. On that day of surrender, Jesus took it all away—the alcohol addiction, the pains of grief in the loss of my daughter. That was the first time I told God I was not mad at Him for her passing, and that if He would help me I wanted to help others to come to know Him better.

After Aaron's passing, I meditated on those words and made a new vow with Him, "Lord please give me the authority of your word to help all to come to you and be saved in your kingdom."

I have never blamed God because of either of their deaths. I am convinced death is not from God. We are told in God's word in Ecclesiastes 3:1-2, **"For everything there is a season, a time for every activity under heaven. A time to be born and a time to die. A time to plant and a time to harvest."** (NLT)

When God first created Heaven and Earth, death was not part of His plan. Every step in the creation was for life. From the first day until the sixth when all creation was made, it was all about beginning, and not an end. God said it was all good! Death came from deception, a lie…from taking our eyes off God, our Creator, and placing our thoughts and minds on creation.

And because of deception, we find in Romans 5:12, **"When Adam sinned, sin entered the world. Adam's sin brought death, so death spread to everyone, for everyone sinned."** (NLT)

I came to the understanding that the devil, who beguiled Adam and Eve in the Garden, is the reason we have to experience death in this world. Romans 6:23: **"For the wages** of sin is death, but the free gift of God is eternal life through Christ Jesus our Lord." (NLT)

The enemy of our souls is the one responsible for bringing death into this world. Not God. Yes, man had a choice, and he chose to follow a lie and not the truth. That is why Jesus Christ came into this world—to correct the deception, to give us His life, and to restore us back into a right relationship with God. Romans 5:18: **"Yes, Adam's one sin brings condemnation for everyone, but Christ's one act of righteousness brings a right relationship with God and new life for everyone."** (NLT)

I thank God for deliverance. I was bound by alcohol, using it to suppress my pain, anger, depression, guilt, and unforgiveness. I thought it would help me be set free from oppressive spirits. Alcohol, drugs, social media, sex, or pornography will not heal you! They only numb you. If they numb you, they will numb your healing, your breakthrough. They are not designed to heal, only to take away from you, to deny the healing you need.

**"He heals the brokenhearted and binds up their wounds" (Psalm 147:3).** This is why I made this vow to God. You may not be a believer in God or the devil, but death is eminent for us all; we all have a date with this destiny. Two destinies we can travel. On one road you have to keep purchasing to fill the void, pain, or emptiness that comes with death. But the other road is free and it is guaranteed to set you free if you allow it to work in your life. John 8:36: **"So if the Son set you free, you are truly free." (NL)**

We all grieve, and we all grieve differently. One reason we grieve is because of our deep love for the life that was taken. Maybe it was our child, sister, brother, mother, father, grandmother, grandfather, uncle, aunt, husband, wife, or friend. We grieve because we miss them. We, who remain alive, have to learn how to process grief, to live without them. Some will isolate themselves from people or society. They will stay away from places and areas that remind them of their loved ones. Maybe it was a tragic death by murder or suicide, which is hard to process. These critical situations can only be helped on the road to healing when you surround yourself with others who have experienced healing from grief. Such is the case with a grief healing class.

I mentioned earlier in this chapter how I experienced peace that surpasses all understanding. One step is to write a letter to God about how you feel and ask Him to help you heal. Write a letter to yourself about your loved one, remembering all the fun and positive times and things you shared together. Make a journal of your healing.

Another step is forgiveness. It's how God guided me on my path to healing. Unforgiveness will impede your healing, causing unnecessary discomfort and pain. It will delay the path to healing. Spiritually, it can—and will—keep you from your salvation. Allowing unforgiveness in our hearts will keep us bound, and in prison.

The parable of the unforgiving debtor found in Matthew 18:21-35 says, **"Then Peter came to him and asked, 'Lord, how often should I forgive someone who sins against me? Seven times?'**

**'No, not seven times,' Jesus replied, 'but seventy times seven! Therefore, the Kingdom of Heaven can be compared to a king who decided to bring his accounts up to date with servants who had borrowed money from him.**

**'In the process, one of his debtors was brought in who owed him millions of dollars. He couldn't pay, so his master ordered that he be sold—along with his wife, his children, and everything he owned—to pay the debt.**

**'But the man fell down before his master and begged him, "Please, be patient with me, and I will pay it all." Then his master was filled with pity for him, and he released him and forgave his debt.**

**'But when the man left the king, he went to a fellow servant who owed him a few thousand dollars. He grabbed him by the throat and demanded instant payment. His fellow servant fell down before him and begged for a little more time. "Be patient with me, and I will pay it," he pleaded. But his creditor wouldn't wait. He had the man**

arrested and put in prison until the debt could be paid in full.

'When some of the other servants saw this, they were very upset. They went to the king and told him everything that had happened. Then the king called in the man he had forgiven and said, "You evil servant! I forgave you that tremendous debt because you pleaded with me. Shouldn't you have mercy on your fellow servant, just as I had mercy on you?"

'Then the angry king sent the man to prison to be tortured until he had paid his entire debt.

'That's what my heavenly Father will do to you if you refuse to forgive your brothers and sisters from your heart.'" (NLT)

In 2015, I made a decision about selling my Big O Tire franchise, that I lament now as I look back upon it. One of my purposes of building that franchise had always been to pass it down to my sons. I rationalized that since I had lost my youngest son, Aaron, and my oldest son, Kevin Jr., didn't want to deal with it, I should sell the business. I listened to the voice of one of my cousins, who convinced me I would do well in another profession. I did so without consulting with God. Today, filled with regret, I now realize how imperative it is to get wise counsel before making any important decisions, especially while in grief.

Eight years have gone by since my son's death, and there is not a moment when I cease thinking about him. I wonder what he would be doing in life. I imagine he would have his own family, and how that would play out. I visit the gravesites of Aaron and Asheli. I often meditate, recalling their lives with positive memories. One day as I sat by the graves, four of Aaron's friends showed up. It was August 20th, the day of his birthday. They told me of how close a friend he was to them, always looking out for and guarding his friends whenever they were threatened. He had a heart for his friends; he became their protector.

Keep positive thoughts for your loved ones. I'm writing this book to let you know that there is a Healer, a Healer who knows everything that we are going through. I know He knows our grief for He grieved also. The Bible says in John 11:35, **"Then Jesus wept."** Weeping for our loved ones is a natural reaction. It's part of our healing, not to be suppressed. Psalm 30:5: **"For his anger lasts for a moment, but his favor lasts a lifetime! Weeping may last through the night, but joy comes with the morning."** (NLT)

I am certain that if we all keep our minds and hearts on Christ, He will guide us step by step to our healing. Even though we will never forget our loved ones, we can be healed of the open wound of grief. He is our salve, our place of restoration, our place of peace.

## Reflection of God's Grace

If you ever doubted whether your loved ones made it into the Kingdom of God, know that the answer is known only by God. We don't know what our Lord spoke to them in the last moment of their lives, and if their hearts were opened to say, "Yes, Lord." The thief on the cross had a change of heart and at that moment he asked Jesus to remember him when He arrives in the kingdom. Jesus replied, "Today you will be with me in Paradise."

The question here is, Are you ready to meet your Lord and Savior? Have you made Jesus the Lord over your life? If your loved one made their home with Jesus, and if you want to see them again, the promise in John 11:25 is for you: **"Jesus told her, 'I am the resurrection and the life. Anyone who believes in Me will live, even after dying.'"** (NLT)

You may not know Jesus. This story is a journey that God has brought me through. These are steps to healing. I asked God that Aaron's and Asheli's deaths would not be in vain, that others would be saved in the Kingdom of God in Heaven, and for us all to see our loved ones again. We have the choice of eternal life with God or eternal death, separated from God and our loved ones forever. All we need is to follow Romans 10:9-10: **"If you openly declare that Jesus is Lord and believe in your heart that God raised Him from the dead, you will be saved. For it is by believing with your heart that you are** made right with God, and by openly declaring your faith that you are saved." (NLT)

Ask God into your heart. Confess Jesus as your Lord and Savior. Ask Him to forgive you of all your sins. Pray this prayer: *"I am a follower of Jesus Christ. My old ways have passed away; all things are new. Thank you, Lord, for all your promises given unto me, guide me now and bless my life. Guide me in my path of redemption and healing, in the precious name of now my Lord and Savior Jesus Christ. Amen and Amen!"*

God has given us a promise to never leave us or forsake us, and that He is coming back to raise our loved ones from the grave, and those who are left to meet him in the air.

Refer to 1 Thessalonians 4:16-17: **"For the Lord himself will come down from heaven with a commanding shout, with the voice of the archangel, and with the trumpet call of God. First, the believers who have died will rise from their graves. Then, together with them, we who are still alive and remain on the earth will be caught up in the clouds to meet the Lord in the air. Then we will be with the Lord forever."** (NLT)

I want to leave us all with the promise of God found in Revelation 21:1-4: **"Then I saw a new heaven and a new earth, for the old heaven and the old earth had disappeared. And the sea was also gone. And I saw the holy city, the new Jerusalem, coming down from God out of heaven like a**

**bride beautifully dressed for her husband. I heard a loud shout from the throne, saying, 'Look, God's home is now among his people! He will live with them, and they will be his people. God himself will be with them. He will wipe every tear from their eyes, and there will be no more death or sorrow or crying or pain. All these things are gone forever.'"** (NLT)

I pray this book will help and guide you through your healing from grief. This journey is not an overnight fix. Grieving takes time, but if you open your heart to our Lord and Savior, He will help guide you to your destiny of having complete peace. It is your choice. I pray God's blessings to all who read this book. His peace I pray over you. May we all make it into Heaven. Amen!

# Epilogue

## Lessons on Lifting the Burdens of Grief

Grief is deep sorrow caused by the death of a loved one. We grieve because we love. Grief is an expression of the love we have for that person. At one point or another, everyone experiences some form of grief.

### The Five Stages of Grief

1. **Denial** – It's a way of trying to minimize the overwhelming pain that someone experiences as they process the reality of their loss. An example of what one might say is, "It doesn't feel real" or "I can't believe they're gone." It may take time for one's mind to adjust to the new reality.

2. **Anger** – One can be angry at God, at close family members, angry at someone who may have caused the death of their loved one or even angry with the person who died.

3. **Bargaining** – Examples of this may be, "God if you bring them back, I'll serve you," or "I promise to be a better person if You let them live." This is a feeling of helplessness and being so desperate that one is willing to do almost anything to avoid the pain of loss.

4. **Depression** – One may experience depression when they've gone through the different stages of grief and the reality of the absence of their loved one begins to set in. There may be feelings of growing sadness, lack of motivation to do simple things like getting out of bed, avoiding people, isolating themselves…etc.

5. **Acceptance** – This is when they are no longer resisting the reality of their loss; they have accepted their "new normal." Even though someone has accepted the reality, it doesn't mean that they no longer have feelings of deep sadness or heartache. It doesn't mean that they no longer cry over their loved one.

God has made each of us unique, so grief will not look the same in every person. Psalm 139:13: **"For you formed my inward parts; you knitted me together in my mother's womb."** (ESV)

One may go through some or all of these stages of grief and they may not experience them in order. There may be no clear defining line when someone is moving from one stage of grief to another. They may also find themselves returning to a stage they already experienced. Along with these different stages of grief, it is common for a person to experience a slew of emotions. They may experience many different emotions all at once.

Grief emotions are not orderly, but instead are more like a tangled ball. There are many more emotions, but here are just a few: anger, annoyance, anxiety, dazedness, bitterness, confusion, disorientation, disappointment, emptiness, broken heartedness, forgetfulness, guilt, numbness, rage, loneliness, and irritability.

## Things _Not_ to Say to Someone Who Is Grieving

*"You have to be strong for your...."*

> This can make a grieving person feel like they're not allowed to show their pain in front of others.
>
> Ecclesiastes 3:4: **"A time to weep and a time to laugh; A time to mourn and a time to dance."** (NASB)

*"God won't give you something you can't handle."*

> When you are experiencing the most intense pain you've ever felt and you hear this statement, it can make you feel like God is uncaring and unloving because He caused you to experience this deep pain.

Lessons on Lifting the Burdens of Grief

*"They're in a better place"*

Try to imagine what a person is feeling while they are grieving the thought of their loved one in a better place. To them the place to be is with them and not gone. We have to be sensitive with our comments, and place ourselves in their position, if possible. It's better to think before we speak.

Let them know that there is hope and the pain they are experiencing will not always feel this intense. Be willing to just listen if they want to talk about their loss. It can be helpful for a grieving person to talk about their loved one, but they may not know how helpful it is until they start talking.

Do pray with them and continue to pray for them after they have left your presence. A grieving person may not have the strength or motivation to pray for themselves. Your prayer may be the only time they get prayed for.

Assure them of God's love for them and that He has not forgotten about them. It may sound so simple but sometimes a grieving person needs to be reminded that God does love them. Psalm 34:18: **"The LORD is close to the brokenhearted and saves those who are crushed in spirit."** (NIV)

Refer them to the GriefShare ministry or any other grief ministry you can recommend. Let them know that it is a place where they will be able to share their own grief experience or just listen to others share theirs. GriefShare is definitely an avenue that God uses to bring healing to the brokenhearted. You can contact them by email: info@griefshare.org or phone: 800 395-5755 or (international) 919 562-2112.

The bottom line is, there is no quick fix to grief. Grief is a process that takes time. For some, it can take weeks, others, months and, as in my case, even years to get to a place of "new normal."

Don't expect that person to be immediately healed when you pray for them or share a Word.

**Ecclesiastes 3: "He has made everything beautiful in its time. Also, he has put eternity into man's heart, yet so that he cannot find out what God has done from the beginning to the end."** (ESV)

## Scriptures That Help in Healing

**"The LORD is close to the brokenhearted. He rescues those whose spirits are crushed."** Psalm 34:18 (NLT)

**"For I can do everything through Christ, who gives me strength."** Philippians 4:13 (NLT)

**"He will wipe every tear from their eyes, and there will be no more death or sorrow or crying or pain. All these things are gone forever."** Revelation 21:4 (NLT)

**"Yet what we suffer now is nothing compared to the glory he will reveal to us later."** Romans 8:18 (NLT)

**"Then Jesus said, "Come to me, all of you who are weary and carry heavy burdens, and I will give you rest. Take my yoke upon you. Let me teach you, because I am humble and gentle at heart, and you will find rest for your souls. For my yoke is easy to bear, and the burden I give you is light."** Matthew 11:28-30 (NLT)

**"Be anxious for nothing, but in everything by prayer and supplication, with thanksgiving, let your requests be made known to God."** Philippians 4:6

**"He heals the brokenhearted; And binds up their wounds."** Psalm 147:3

**"Therefore, you now have sorrow; but I will see you again and your heart will rejoice, and your joy no one will take from you."** John 16:22

**"My flesh and my heart may fail, but God is the rock and strength of my heart and my portion forever."** Psalm 73:26

## If You Know Someone in Crisis

Call the National Suicide Prevention Lifeline (Lifeline) at 1-800-273-TALK (8255), or text the Crisis Text Line (text HELLO to 741741). Both services are free and available 24 hours a day, seven days a week. The deaf and hard of hearing can contact the Lifeline via TTY at 1-800-799-4889. All calls are confidential. Contact social media outlets directly if you are concerned about a friend's social media updates or dial 911 in an emergency. Learn more on the Lifeline's website or the Crisis Text Line's website.

The Veterans Crisis Line connects Service members and Veterans in crisis, as well as their family members and friends, with qualified, caring Department of Veteran's Affairs (VA) responders through a confidential toll-free hotline, online chat, or text messaging service. Dial 1-800-273-8255 and Press 1 to talk to someone or send a text message to 838255 to connect with a VA responder. You can also start a confidential online chat session at veteranscrisisline.net/get-help/chat.

## Five Steps You Can Take To Be the One to Help Someone in Emotional Pain

The National Suicide Prevention Lifeline offers these steps you can take:

**1. ASK:** "Are you thinking about killing yourself?" It's not an easy question, but studies show that asking at-risk individuals if they are suicidal does not increase suicides or suicidal thoughts.

**2. KEEP THEM SAFE:** Reducing a suicidal person's access to highly lethal items or places is an important part of suicide prevention. While this is not always easy, asking if the at-risk person has a plan and removing or disabling the lethal means can make a difference.

**3. BE THERE:** Listen carefully and learn what the individual is thinking and feeling. Research suggests acknowledging and talking about suicide may reduce rather than increase suicidal thoughts.

**4. HELP THEM CONNECT:** Save the National Suicide Prevention Lifeline's (1-800-273-TALK (8255)) and the Crisis Text Line's number (741741) in your phone, so it's there when you need it. You can also help make a connection with a trusted individual like a family member, friend, spiritual advisor, or mental health professional.

**5. STAY CONNECTED:** Staying in touch after a crisis or after being discharged from care can make a difference. Studies have shown the number of suicide deaths goes down when someone follows up with the at-risk person.

## Author's Biographical Sketch

Kevin G. Ellison, Sr. was born in Los Angeles, California. His family moved to Riverside when he was 1 year old. He was raised in Riverside most of his life. He joined the Seventh-day Adventist church in his later years, and became an ordained elder within the denomination.

Kevin was blessed to have served in the automotive repair business for over 38 years, working for a prominent tire franchise that served multiple dealerships in the US. He served as a store manager, trainer, motivator, franchise owner in a joint partnership, and then sole owner. After selling his tire franchise, he became a licensed life and health insurance agent, helping people to prepare for their retirement and future.

Kevin eventually started attending a non-denominational church in San Bernardino, California. He was blessed to become a leader for the Child Dedication Department. His passion is to help people who have gone through or are experiencing grief. The church later started a grief ministry, of which he became the leader of this much needed ministry.

During his time at the church, the church started Leadership University, in which he was part of the first graduating class in 2019, earning degrees in Leadership, Evangelism, Biblical Studies, and Theology. In 2020 he was asked to help teach the Evangelism 101 class for the evening students. His passion is helping people in every facet of business and church affiliation, and guiding people to receive the ultimate goal of eternal life, which is in Christ Jesus. His wish is that the lives of those he touches be filled with the peace and love of God.

Author's Biographical Sketch

## Author's Contact Information

Connect with me on Twitter: @KevinGEllison51

Connect with me on Facebook:
https://www.facebook.com/kevin.g.ellison

https://www.facebook.com/Unearned-Grief-The-Hearts-Journey-From-Pain-To-Peace-105777184994925

Connect with me on Instagram:
https://www.instagam.com/ellisonkevin/

Connect with me on LinkedIn:
https://www.linkedin.com/kevin-ellison-902b19b4/